Design
with
Japanese
Obi

Obi

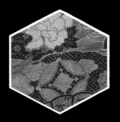

Diane
Wiltshire
and
Ann
Wiltshire

Charles E. Tuttle Company
Rutland, Vermont & Tokyo, Japan

(Frontispiece) *An ornate maru obi is strewn over a soft blanket of snow.*

Published by the Charles E. Tuttle Company, an imprint of Periplus Editions (HK) Ltd. Editorial offices at 2-6 Suido 1-chome, Bunkyo-ku, Tokyo 112. © 1997 by Charles E. Tuttle Publishing Company, Inc. All rights reserved. LCC Card No. 96-61005. ISBN 0-8048-2070-8. First edition, 1997.

Printed in Singapore

Visit Tuttle Web on the Internet at:
http://www.tuttle.co.jp/~tuttle/

Contents

Acknowledgments

*In loving memory of
our mother and grandmother,
Linda Brumfield Bilbo*

Special thanks are in order to the many people whose advice and support enabled us to write a book about decorating with the Japanese obi. At Tuttle, our editor provided the initial enthusiasm for the project and then proceeded to implement and refine our vision. Our Australian photographer, Vincent Long, worked tirelessly in the U.S. and Tokyo to give us the shots that we needed. Thanks also to Michael Barrett and Michael Guttuso for providing us with additional photographs and styling. In Tokyo, Barbara Knode introduced us to the design genius of Shoji Osugi and we spent a delightful day together photographing his exquisite obi creations. Naomi Iwasaki Hoff graciously provided us with her original obi pillows and teaboxes for use in the book. A big thank you goes to Martha Widman for her fine sewing skills; Martha has relined or repaired hundreds of obi for us over the years and her handiwork is featured in many of the obi pillow designs shown in this book. We also appreciate the hours that Noriko Faust spent translating the tiny *kanji* (Chinese characters) on the back of obi for us. In Washington D.C., the staff at the Textile Museum was invaluable in contributing to our research. Additional information was obtained by consulting with the many obi experts in Japan who patiently answered our endless questions. We especially want to thank Gallery Kawano and Toshiko Yamazaki, Shigeko Ikeda, Seizaburo Ando at Odawara Shoten, Yukiko Matsuzaki, Yoshiko Chida, Ryoko Masakane, Naiko Funakoshi, Aiko Sasaki, Setsuko Miura, and the Nishijin-ori Kai in Kyoto. And to those friends who so generously opened their homes to us for photographing the obi in all manner of settings, a very special thank you!

In Japan
Sabine and Urs Schmid, Kathryn and Curtis Baker, Barbara and Don Knode, Geeta and Krishen Mehta, Ellen and David Dutkowsky, Linda and John Farrell, Ivan Woodhouse, Naomi Iwasaki Hoff

In the U.S.
Connie and Steve Lanzl, Loralie and Lee Parks, Sarah and Phil Nelson, Joanne and Philip Horton, Susan Kasper, Gerald Falls, Lee and Dick Nance, Carol O'Donnell Miscio at Celestial Connections

Introduction
Using Obi as a Decorative Accessory

Over the past few decades the Japanese kimono sash, or *obi*, has gained popularity as a home decorating accessory. The exquisite silk fabric, made into intricate patterns with stunning colors, makes the obi desirable as an accent in any room. Any of the obi styles mentioned in this book can be turned into objects of art for the home. Unlike the rules of fashion that dictate which kimono are worn with which obi, there are no restrictions when it comes to decorating with the obi. From contemporary to traditional interiors, the draping of an obi in a room can soften hard lines and add color to an otherwise drab area.

Although the most popular use for the obi with Westerners is as a table runner, it can also be used as a wall hanging or sculpture, or as an accent on furniture such as chests, pianos, and mantels. Obi of varying lengths can be folded, knotted, or tied with tassels to achieve the desired effect. Remnants of silk obi can be resewn into pillows and bedspreads, even showcased in picture frames.

Initially the *maru obi* was favored as an accessory due to its length of up to 4 m (4$\frac{1}{2}$ yd.) and width usually of 30 cm (12 in.). Maru obi also tend to be made of the finest brocade and are more expensive than other styles. *Fukuro obi,* while sewn differently, are very similar to maru obi in length and width. As fukuro obi were introduced in the 1920s in Japan, the very oldest obi are almost always of the maru style.

When selecting either a maru or fukuro obi, take time to unfold the obi and check the full length for any damaged spots. Also, look carefully at the design, as some obi may be missing part of the pattern. You may find, for example, that the flowers in a pattern are not fully colored on one section. This may have been an economic decision and not an oversight as only certain sections of the obi are visible when worn with kimono. However for someone who plans to display the full length, an uneven or unfinished pattern could present a problem.

Check the reverse side of the obi as well. Many obi are reversible, with a different but equally fantastic design on the back. It may also be a less expensive piece of fabric that totally clashes with the front. Sometimes the lining is plain silk, or perhaps a satin weave, and occasionally there may be no silk lining but a cheap, gauze-like fabric instead. Many obi sold for use in interiors have a new, neutral lining sewn on the back, especially if the original lining was unattractive or damaged.

Although the *Nagoya* style is a bit shorter, 314–345 cm (124–136 in.), than the formal maru or fukuro obi, it is quite popular for use in decorating due to its wide range of colors. Because it is pre-folded and easier to tie, the Nagoya obi is a convenient choice for young Japanese women to wear with kimono. This explains the availability of richer and brighter hues in the Nagoya style, as these colors are more appropriate for young or unmarried women.

In its original form, with part of the obi folded over and stitched, the Nagoya obi has a unique asymmetrical line. This seam can also be opened and the obi relined in order to achieve a longer style. If the obi is fully patterned, then it is easy to unstitch the seam, open it and reline the fabric. Before attempting this, check the folded area to see if the fabric is worn. Most obi will show a slight crease down the middle when they are opened, but, if the fabric is too worn, it will appear damaged.

If your Nagoya obi has a design on only sixty percent of the material, the plain portion can be cut out and the patterned pieces fitted together and resewn. Although this results in a shorter obi of approximately 213 cm (84.1 in.), the length is often more suitable for placing on the top of a small chest or table. Used in the original form, without relining, it is easy to knot or fold the narrow end of a Nagoya obi, whether patterned or plain, for a special touch.

Obi in the *hanhaba* fashion are very much in demand, due to their affordable price and narrow width of 15 cm (6 in.). This size is ideal for accenting the top of a mantel or for draping along the narrow stairs of a step chest *(kaidan dansu)*. Another popular use for the hanhaba is as a wall hanging. The width is almost identical to that of old-fashioned "bell pulls," which hung in the homes of wealthy families, especially in the southern United States in the late nineteenth and early twentieth centuries. These bell pulls, made of elegant tapestry, were mounted with brass fittings at the top and bottom.

Seasonal colors and motifs that are so important in all aspects of Japanese life, from culture and design to food and clothing, are also evident in obi. When creating a spring table setting you may want to use an obi in soft pink shades, perhaps sprinkled with embroidered cherry blossoms. For a festive holiday look, obi in bright reds and deep greens add elegance to any interior. Dramatic autumn shades of orange and rust are also color schemes frequently found in the obi.

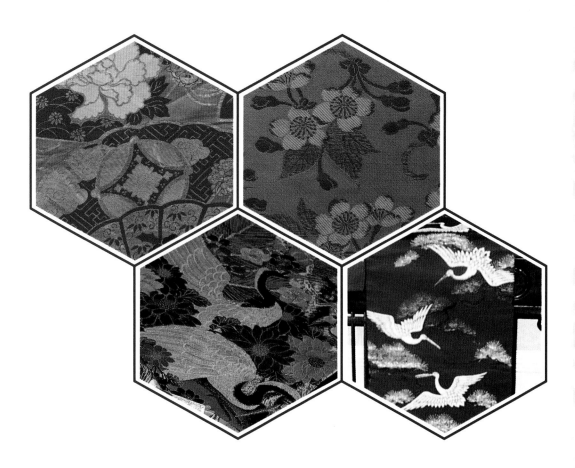

When buying an obi for use as a decorative accent in the home, coordinating with your interior colors is the most important consideration. Though an obi in good condition will have a higher value, the condition alone is not the most critical factor. Slight stains and worn spots will not detract from an obi in the perfect color, with an exquisite design, used in the ideal setting.

Certain symbols and motifs are more popular than others in obi designs. The crane, a symbol of long life, appears frequently, usually in white on a colored background. Other good luck symbols include the pine bough, bamboo branch, and phoenix. Frequently a particular flower or tree is paired with a particular bird. For example, the phoenix, peacock, fowl, and pheasant are usually shown with the peony, while the crane is often shown together with pine.

Other popular designs include the Japanese fan; cherry, plum, and peach blossoms; and the Imperial family's crest, the chrysanthemum. Many stunning obi have a repeat pattern of family crests, or *mon*, covering the obi. Some of the most popular obi designs were brought from China hundreds of years ago, in particular the geometric designs which are based on ancient Chinese patterns. Other common Chinese themes in obi design are *koma-inu* (lion-dogs), dragons, and other animals.

Because the obi, due to the impracticality of wearing kimono, may have lost its place as the central element in Japanese wardrobes, these works of art have found their way into the hands of new owners who cherish the obi's beauty and history. From contemporary to classic, traditional to eclectic, interiors of every genre can be accented with obi in various guises. There is no right or wrong way to use an obi as a decorating accessory, and the obi fabrics lend themselves to a wide variety of applications. As the following photographs will illustrate, imaginative obi creations can add a dramatic effect to any room.

Each obi is unique and, with proper care, will appreciate in value as time goes by. Just as Japanese women traditionally passed their obi down from mother to daughter, so will a new generation of families pass down their treasured obi heirlooms.

Table Art

Japanese obi take on a life of their own when used to enhance a coffee table, still life, or floral arrangement. Obi fabric has body and weight which lends itself beautifully to all manner of twists, ties and angles. Don't be afraid to experiment with knots and bows, the creases usually fall out easily.

One of the most striking statements in a room can come from an obi placed strategically on a coffee table. You will see several examples of this on the following pages where the obi adds a dash of drama and interest to glass, wood, or marble surfaces.

Festive colors such as red, green, and gold are actually quite common in the obi; as a result many people own at least one "holiday" obi which can be used on a table or mantel, or

A rust-and-gold Nagoya obi with navy blue accents combines dramatically with an autumn flower arrangement.

*This gift shop uses a festive maru obi in red and gold colors
to highlight their Christmas display.*

A gold, red, and black fukuro obi on a red-lacquered kimono stand. The blank section is cleverly concealed so that only the ornate iris design is shown.

Here, a white obi floats within a glass-covered coffee table. The splashes of deep red in the simple obi design pick up the burgundy color scheme of the living room.

Wrapped around a pot of geraniums, a maru obi with a touch of red brightens up a corner of this room.

Note the intricate fan design using gold threads on black silk.

*The complementary blue and orange hues in this Nagoya obi
create a gentle still life.*

Dining Accents

Probably the most popular use for the Japanese obi in Western interiors is incorporating them in table settings. Whether you display a grand maru obi down the full length of a formal dinner table or make creative use of an asymmetrical Nagoya obi, nothing else makes quite the statement that an obi does as the perfect dining accent.

An obi can be easily adjusted in length to suit almost any table. Note the variety of ripples, folds, and knots in the following photographs; these allow even the longest obi to fit a shorter table. Additional accents can include candles, flowers, tassels, a small sculpture, or favorite objet d'art.

Treat your obi as you would your fine table linens; most food stains should be sent to the dry cleaner for treatment. Candle wax can be scraped off once dry, but, depending on the color of the obi, the mark may remain. Obviously, the more colorful and ornate the obi pattern, the less likely it is that a slight stain will show.

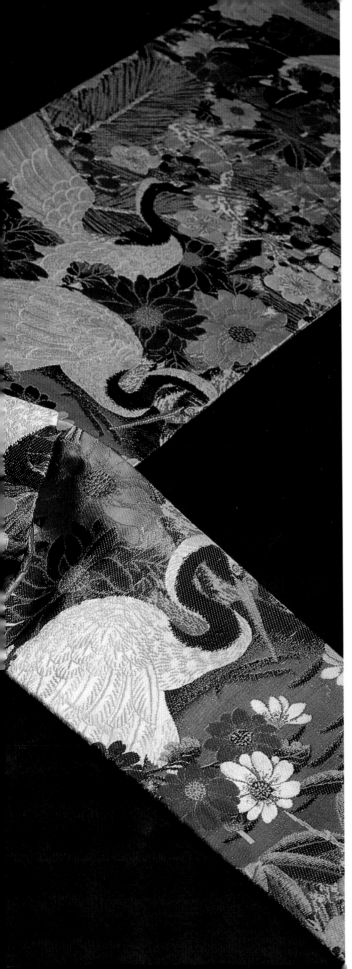

A heavily embroidered obi featuring white cranes echoes the same design in the Fitz and Floyd dinner plates.

Note the interesting effect created by leaving the plain end of the Nagoya obi unfinished, then tying a knot for a dramatic asymmetrical look.

A peach- and gold-silk fukuro obi accents the contemporary California look of this living room.

Here we have a simple but striking table setting with dancing Chinese lions embroidered on a black-silk fukuro obi.

A summer setting for lunch on a low Japanese table with a pink-and-blue color scheme reflected in the maru obi.

This striking Nagoya obi brings life to a creative table setting.

(Detail) Note that because of the folded style and the stiffness of the fabric, Nagoya obi can easily be pinched into dramatic shapes.

A child's hanhaba obi is a festive addition to this birthday-party table setting.

Framing Highlights

Certain types of obi lend themselves well to being accents for photographs, mirrors or artwork; in some cases, the obi itself becomes the work of art.

In this chapter, you will see how the narrow hanhaba style provides the perfect backdrop for several prints. Narrower obi are also easier to drape or tie above mirrors. In a sense, the obi in this case returns to its original function of setting off or highlighting the colors and textures of another work of art.

Obi fragments can be used to accent a picture frame; larger pieces matted and framed become stunning works of art in themselves. Framing a section of obi is an especially good idea when the fabric is delicate or quite old. A rare Nagoya obi, such as the Golden Pavilion scene depicted in this chapter, may be best displayed within a window-box type frame.

This exquisite picture frame is fashioned from blue silk material accented with bits of obi fabric on the corners.

Cranes and chrysanthemums in soft shades of mauve nestle among the forest-green pine in this framed wall tapestry.

A matching pair of obi panels are framed and placed side by side.

Here, a woodblock print is suspended over a hanhaba obi in similar colors. First, a portion of the obi is knotted to achieve the desired length, then the top and middle sections of the obi are tacked to the wall, and finally the picture is hung in place.

This very special obi has a scene of Kyoto's famed Golden Pavilion delicately embroidered with silk threads on a black-silk background. The Nagoya obi is folded in such a way that the design is most prominent and it has been mounted in a shadow box for a stunning effect.

(Detail) The tiny silk stitches make the scene appear to have been painted by hand.

Festive gold reindeer adorn the top of this sideboard. Two obi are combined, one framed and the other as a table runner, both in holiday reds and golds.

(Detail) A closer look at obi with golden threads and shimmering reds—very popular for decorating during the holiday season.

A soft pink hanhaba obi is perched on top of an oval gilt mirror, bringing color and interest to the room.

Draping Effects

Wall hangings, headboards, even window treatments are some of the possibilities when decorating with the Japanese obi. Using lacquer poles, bamboo rods, or brass bars, it is relatively simple to drape the obi in a way that features its spectacular design. In giving the obi display a horizontal orientation rather than a vertical hanging, attention will be focused a bit more on the room itself, as the viewer's eye will be attracted to a wider area.

Don't limit yourself to hanging obi in a straight line; experiment with various angles. The addition of tassels or knots, while not necessary, can add elegance and interest to the design.

After achieving the desired drape, you may need to secure the folds of the obi to the wall with a small thumbtack or nail. Another option is to baste the folds into place. The support bar can be secured with nails or hooks.

The navy blue underside of this fukuro obi adds depth and beauty to a window treatment.

An obi, draped together with sudare (bamboo blinds),
provides a dramatic headboard effect for this bedroom.
The narrow width of a hanhaba obi makes it quite flexible
for draping or tying.

An unusual double-obi arrangement flies above this bed. Using a black lacquer hanger with brass fittings, the rod is suspended at a slight angle. After draping a simply decorated burgundy obi, a more ornate fan-design obi in shades of burgundy and green was added.

A vibrant blue Nagoya obi is suspended from a worn bamboo pole.

This simple black Nagoya obi speaks of celebration with its bright plum blossoms and origami cranes. The black lacquer pole is actually intended for hanging a kimono, but has been adjusted for the obi.

A crimson dragon motif embroidered on teal damask makes an interesting wall hanging for this fukuro obi.

In this home, we see a stenciled silk fukuro obi suspended from a bamboo pole and then knotted and draped across an ornate stone table.

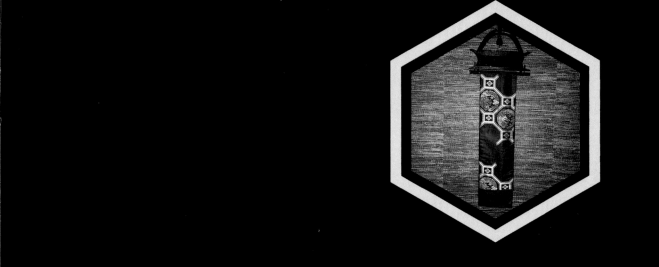

Hanging Displays

There is no better way to fill an empty wall space than with a magnificent silk obi hanging. Especially for those hard-to-fit, sky-high spaces such as stairwells, the obi is a great decorating choice. Here, the viewer's eye will be drawn vertically, and dramatic spaces in the home or office can be made truly spectacular. Again, the supporting rod can be made of wood, brass, or another sturdy material. Sometimes a double rod is necessary to properly display a very long obi.

Antique Thai loom hangers—works of art in and of themselves—are much in demand as a simple method of hanging an obi on the wall. You will see an example of this hanger in the following chapter. The recycled looms come in two widths; the widest can hold up to three obi vertically or one placed horizontally. Both styles are ideal for headboards.

The old Burmese loom hanger is an ideal way to display an obi.
The obi was originally in the fukuro style, but the blank part of
the design has been cut out, leaving only the striking pattern
of fans and flowers.

Embroidered silk cranes in brilliant hues give a three-dimensional effect to this exquisite gold fukuro obi.

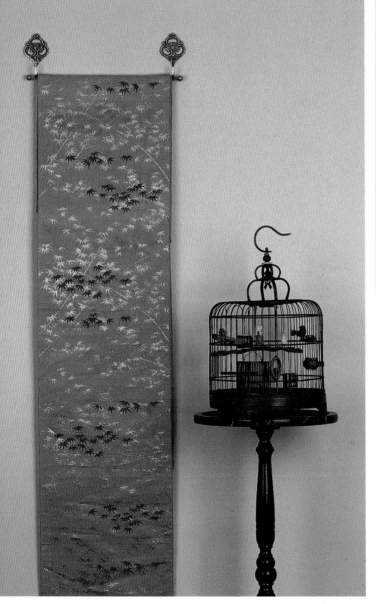

Autumn is evident in this sand-colored silk fukuro obi sprinkled with gold- and rust-colored maple leaves.

An elegant maru obi, in deep green with gold embroidered medallions, accents this bedroom ensemble. The obi has been cut into two pieces and used for the wall-hanging headboard design as well as for the bedside table runner.

A length of obi in gold and olive tones provides the backdrop
for this collection of antique combs mounted on Japanese
sudare (bamboo blinds), as designed by Shoji Osugi.

Furniture Complements

In this chapter we hope to introduce even more ideas for using the Japanese obi in your home. From the smallest chest to the tallest highboy, any piece of furniture is enhanced by the addition of an obi. Notice how austere settings are brightened up, color schemes are tied together, and hard lines are softened with the proper placement of an obi. Depending on the technique chosen, the results can range from subdued to striking. Here, as with framing, the obi works in conjunction with its surroundings in a dynamic way.

If an obi is too wide or stiff to knot, a similar effect can be achieved with the use of a rubber band. The gathered section can then be covered with a silk tassel or braided rope. Don't feel limited to keeping your obi in one spot; experiment with moving your obi collection around to different pieces of furniture for a fresh look.

Shades of blue and gray in this summer obi highlight the antique Asian silver collection.

Splashes of rust and teal reflect the colors of the print on the wall and the ikebana *flower arrangement* as the long maru obi flows across a Japanese tansu, or chest.

A view of the coordinating maru obi draped across an old Japanese chest.

A maru obi in pastel tones hides the chipped finish on the top of this Japanese chest. Notice the puddling effect as the obi trails gracefully onto the floor.

A pink and blue Hakata obi embraces this spring flowerpot and accents the collection of blue-and-white porcelain.

This brocade Nagoya obi is displayed with its original folds intact, creating a striking pattern to enhance the art work above.

This reversible maru obi (note the different design on the underside) is placed in a dramatic position to highlight the Roy Fairchild painting above.

Kokeshi dolls find a resting place atop this imposing chest. A colorful Nagoya obi harmonizes and softens the scene.

A woven obi picks up the colors of the Japanese wood-block print and forms a stage for the antique iron teapot collection.

65

Lively blue waves dance down this summer obi placed on top of nesting tables. The swirl design is similar to the Vietnamese carving used as a lamp base.

This one-hundred-year-old maru obi featuring a butterfly design is doubled and draped across a Chinese trunk.

An antique fukuro obi in pastel shades caresses the top of a baby grand piano.

The elegance of gold and white cranes adorn this fukuro obi draped atop an upright piano.

The use of this maru obi enhances a display of antique Japanese imari.

A colorful maru obi dresses up a Japanese step chest (kaidan dansu).

This lightweight summer obi in brilliant teal blue brightens up a stair banister.

(Detail) A vibrant red obi cord anchors the obi to the banister with a dash of color. Note how the embroidered medallions dress up the simple gauze weave.

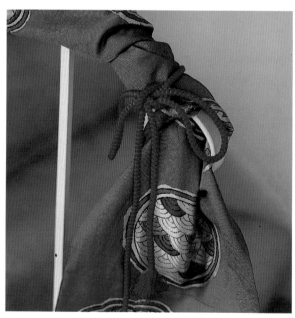

Notice how the colors of the obi coordinate perfectly with the Tibetan painting above.

(Detail) An ornate but slightly narrow maru obi adds elegance to this mantel setting. The size of this obi makes it a perfect fit.

The use of an obi here adds color and interest to the scene.

Fabric Coverings

Obi fabric is ideal for making cushions and pillows, but in this section we will present additional options, such as using obi remnants as coverings for tea boxes, chairs, even walls.

These are ideal solutions for using that exquisite obi which happens to be permanently stained. Cut up and recycle as many pieces of the silk as you can. As the obi changes its natural shape and form, the creative uses to which it can be employed expand tremendously.

When considering a piece of obi for upholstery, make sure it is sturdy enough to withstand everyday use. As you will see in the following photographs, there are many different styles of obi pillows. If you have a narrow piece of obi material, you may want to surround it with a border in order to achieve the desired size. Again, take care when selecting an obi to make into a pillow; the older, more fragile pieces will fall apart.

These brocade pillows are covered on
both sides with remnants of obi material.

Note the different designs, one with a blue velvet border, the smaller one without, and both accented by silk tassels.

Black-and-gold obi-pillows by Naomi Iwasaki Hoff add a dramatic flair to this suede sofa.

An obi pillow designed by Naomi Iwasaki Hoff uses a rectangular piece of obi framed by ivory silk fabric, and is accented with black piping.

Pillows inset with squares of fine obi brocade add elegance to any interior.

Here, Tokyo Designer Shoji Osugi transformed two small wood hibachi (grills) into petite stools with the addition of obi-covered cushions.

The rich obi brocade with a fan design lends a Japanese touch to the Western-style chair.

Shoji Osugi chose a traditional obi fabric for covering these dining room chairs. The rich color and design of the obi is the perfect complement to the fan-carved table.

The rusted inner lining of this old Kyoto-style hibachi took on new life with a liner made of soft antique obi silk. Design by Shogi Osugi.

One end of a Nagoya obi is cleverly placed on top of this piano bench, with the excess section tucked inside.

A section of maru obi has been sewn across this collapsible lacquer stool to create a unique design, for use as either a luggage rack or small bench.

With the addition of a glass top, the obi stool can also be used as a decorative table.

This tea box is covered in persimmon-colored raw silk and trimmed with remnants of the obi from the step chest (kaidan dansu) in the background. By opening the obi's side seam the maru hanhaba becomes wide enough to decorate the top of the chest; the remaining narrow piece makes a nice border.

Naomi Iwasaki Hoff's tea-box design, covered in silk fabric and obi pieces, makes an unusual end table.

Shoji Osugi created a stunning effect with this small Japanese chest. A gilt obi pattern of bamboo makes a showpiece out of a plain tansu.

A magnificent four-panel screen is created by cutting a maru obi into four pieces and adhering them to the folding surface.

Here, Shoji Osugi has inserted a quiet gold obi material on either side of the ranma (transom window) hanging above the large chest. The worn rice paper lining on the chest's small sliding cabinets has been replaced with obi fabric as well.

To create this very special bedspread, two identical maru obi were stitched into place.

History of the Obi

The earliest obi was more functional than ornate. In the Heian period (794–1185), the first obi consisted of a narrow sash used to hold up culotte-like pants called *hakama*. This undergarment was covered by layers of unlined kimono, so that the obi was not visible.

Later, after the Muromachi period, (1392–1573), women of the samurai class began tying their obi on the outside of their garments, usually knotted in the front or on the side. During this time the *uchikake,* or long outer coat, became popular, and, although the obi was visible, it was overshadowed by the decorative uchikake.

By the Momoyama period, (1573–1615), the obi was slightly wider and sometimes made of silk, with plaids and checks being popular patterns. An optional obi style consisted of a braided fabric with tassels added to each end. This narrow braided obi was then wrapped around the waist and tied with dangling knots. Largely ornamental, the braided, tasseled obi never really caught on.

Traditional clothing of the Edo period, (1600–1868), included the kimono and obi as we know them today. Then, as now, the obi was necessary to keep the kimono securely closed in front (over other fasteners that hold the garment together). By the middle of the Edo period, obi measurements were standardized to 360 cm by 26.8 cm (142 in. by 11 in.).

Edo fashion was influenced by courtesans and entertainers of the age. Women of the samurai class continued to wear the simpler *kosode* kimono tied together with an obi made of braided cords. Outside the samurai class women experimented with more elaborate kimono, the *furisode* style, often seen on the Kabuki stage. Characterized by long, flowing sleeves, the furisode kimono was accented by a large, loosely-tied obi.

For many years all styles of obi were usually tied at the front or on the side, but the back position became the more accepted form by the mid-Edo period. It is said that this rear style originated in the mid-1700s when a Kabuki actor, imitating a young girl, came on stage with his obi tied in the back. Another reason for the change may have been that the sheer bulk of the wider obi became too cumbersome for tying in the front.

Even though the obi was becoming an important part of a woman's ensemble, it was not until the middle of the Edo period that it became as prominent as the kimono. It was then that designers, weavers, and dyers all focused their talents on creating longer, wider, and more elaborate obi.

The Meiji era, (1868–1912), witnessed a revolution in the textile industry with the advent of electric weaving looms and chemical dying techniques from the West. During this time women's kimono ceased to be worn in the free-flowing style of earlier days. The new fashion was to tuck them at the waist so that the length of the kimono could be adjusted in accordance with a woman's height. These tucks and folds were visible and became part of the art of tying the obi. Obi were sometimes made shorter than before, with the most popular bow being the simple *taiko musubi*, or drum bow.

As for the men's obi, or *otoko obi*, the earliest styles were simple and functional, much like the women's. For a short time during the Edo period, men experimented with wider obi made of more exotic fabrics, but this fashion did not last. After expanding to the current width of 10–15 cm (4–6 in.), men's obi became much more subdued in color and design. Even today, you will see very little design on a man's obi, with the exception of a fringe trim or interesting weave.

Note: The hexagonal tortoise-shell motif, used through out this book, is a popular Japanese design element that symbolizes longevity and good fortune.

Weaves, Dyes, Stitches

The vast majority of all the obi produced in Japan today come from a district in Kyoto known as Nishijin. This area is filled with hundreds of workshops where weavers labor at their looms, about a fourth of which are still hand-operated. Since the 15th century, Nishijin has been the center of the Japanese textile industry. Initially famous for brocades, twills, and gauzes produced on draw looms, Nishijin switched to Jacquard looms in the late 1800s after a team of its weavers returned from France with the new technique.

The high-quality brocade obi produced by the Nishijin artisans is known as *nishiki,* meaning "beautiful color combination." It is characterized by the lavish use of gold and silver threads with patterns of flowers, birds, or ancient geometrical designs. Another style of elaborate obi manufactured in Nishijin is the *tsuzure,* or tapestry weave. Both brocade and tapestry obi are the most ornate and expensive of all obi.

Lightweight obi are made using an open weave, resulting in a gauze-like material, commonly referred to as *karami ori.* These are worn mostly in warm weather or with a casual kimono. A distinctive silk weave, also popular in the summer, is the *Hakata obi.* Named for the area of Kyushu where it originated, Hakata obi are characterized by their series of woven stripes.

Any unlined obi woven in one piece may be referred to as *hitoe.* This word literally means "one layer" and is also used to describe unlined kimono. *Hara-awase* is a term used when speaking of a double-sided obi that has a different fabric on the underside, usually black or white. This reversible style enables the wearer to enjoy two different designs with one obi.

Other weaves used in the making of obi are satin weave, or *shusu,* which creates a smooth lustrous surface, and damask weave, or *donsu,* which results in a pattern on both sides. The thickest weave, usually in a rough plaid or stripe is *saka ori.* Saka-ori obi are narrow in width and are worn only with cotton kimono, never silk. The *kinran* weave, brought to Japan from China, is made by sewing a simple gold motif on a plain background.

Any design or weave which reflects a Chinese influence is called *kara ori.*

In addition to weaving, other methods of obi decoration employ dyeing techniques such as stenciling, or painting by hand. Sometimes a

unique process of adhering gold or silver leaf to the silk is also used in obi design. The *Yuzen* method, producing a hand-painted dyed design using rice paste, was perfected by the middle of the seventeenth century. A Kyoto fan-maker, Miyasaki Yuzensai, developed this revolutionary technique which enabled much thinner lines to be drawn on the cloth, resulting in more intricate designs. Embroidery is often used together with weaving or dyeing to enhance the beauty of an obi.

Japanese embroidery consists of several different stitches, primarily the satin stitch, split stitch, and couching stitch. The couching stitch is much longer than the other two; cotton thread used in couching may be covered in gold or silver foil for an especially elegant look. A variation on the French knot is also used to add more depth and color to an obi design.

On the underside of an obi you may notice delicately embroidered *kanji* (Chinese characters) at one end. Usually these kanji are the signature of the shop where the obi was made. If the designer of the obi was especially famous, then his name, instead of the textile maker's, may appear in kanji. Sometimes the embroidery will include the shop or family crest in addition to the row of kanji. Often the embroidery is hidden just inside the end seam of the obi where it is not noticeable unless the seam is opened.

Poems, such as the one in the beginning of this book, are also found embroidered on the lining of obi. These poems tend to be simple Japanese *haiku*, but Buddhist prayers, elaborately embroidered, are used as well. Even the front side of some obi may be covered in kanji; when used as the main decorative feature, the embroidery is probably that of a well-known ancient poem or prayer.

Once in a while you may see intricate stitches sewn onto the obi in appliqué form. These minute stitches, known as the blind stitch or forbidden stitch, are actually pieces of Chinese embroidery which were brought to Japan, cut up, and then added to the obi. The tiny knots could only be made by a child's hands using the slave labor that was supposedly outlawed in China toward the end of the nineteenth century.

Today, even though Japanese obi are more popular than ever in elegant homes from New York to Sydney, the decline of the kimono industry in Japan has led to fewer and fewer obi being produced each year. For several decades now Japanese women have found Western dress more practical, comfortable, and economical than traditional Japanese kimono and obi. The trousseau of fine heirloom obi are no longer a part of most women's lives. They make do with the one or two obi and kimono that they may own, or resort to rental services for special occasions such as weddings or coming-of-age celebrations.

While the Japanese favor handing down their obi to family members, you will not find much enthusiasm for recycling and wearing second-hand obi and kimono. The feeling is that something of the wearer's spirit remains in the clothing and could perhaps result in bad luck. This belief is based on doctrines of the Buddhist religion.

Although the Japanese traditionally have had a thrifty approach to getting the most wear or service out of any object, this philosophy does not extend to the concept of obi as a decorating accessory. To the Japanese the obi is strictly regarded as part of the kimono attire, not something to drape across a table!

Types of Obi

The Japanese obi can be divided into four basic categories.

The most formal is the maru obi. Usually made of elaborately patterned brocade or tapestry and decorated with many gold threads, the maru obi was most popular during the Meiji and Taisho eras. Nowadays it is almost obsolete due to its uncomfortable weight and exorbitant cost. With the exception of weddings and other very formal occasions, the maru obi is rarely worn today.

There is only one seam on a maru obi as the fabric is doubled over length-wise and sewn together along one side. It consists of up to 420 cm (165 in.) of fine material with a total width of up to 68 cm (27 in.), although the finished piece is usually 30–33 cm (12–13 in.) wide when folded. A stiff lining can often be found in old obi.

Even though the classic maru obi measures a width of 33 cm (13 in.), the maru-obi style appears in narrower widths as well. One reason for the more narrow width in an obviously very fine maru obi may be that it was custom-made slightly narrower for a petite client.

Slightly less formal than the maru obi is the fukuro (double-fold or pocket) obi. This style of obi was created in the late 1920s; supposedly the first one was exhibited in Mitsukoshi department store in 1927. The fabric is again a fine brocade or tapestry, but the construction of the fukuro obi makes it less bulky to work with than a maru obi.

A *hon-fukuro* (true double-fold) obi is an obi that was actually woven in the pillowcase style with no seam. The more common *nui-fukuro obi* refers to two panels woven separately and then stitched together in a pillowcase or pocket style. The finished fukuro obi is the same length and width as most maru obi, and when tied over kimono, the fukuro obi can hardly be distinguished from the maru style. The back of this obi may be lined with a plain silk or brocade, making it less expensive than the full maru obi. The front side is either sixty percent or fully patterned, and although not quite as ceremonial as a maru obi, the fukuro obi is acceptable for formal occasions.

The most convenient kind of obi for today's Japanese woman is the Nagoya obi, first produced in the city of Nagoya at the end of the Taisho era, (1912–26). Lighter and simpler than the fukuro or maru obi, the Nagoya obi is characterized by a portion of the obi being pre-folded and stitched in half. The narrow part wraps around the waist, and the wider piece forms the bow in back. Close observation will reveal that, when worn, a Nagoya

obi is tied with a single fold, whereas a maru or fukuro obi, being longer, is tied in a double fold. The majority of Nagoya obi are much less expensive than their longer counterparts and tend to be made of cheaper fabrics. Nevertheless, their designs and colors can be stunning.

The hanhaba obi, so named because it is half the width of other obi, is usually 15 cm (6 in.) wide. A more casual style of obi, the hanhaba is suitable for wearing with kimono at home, under a *haori* (kimono coat), or with children's kimono. Usually the fabric and design of these obi reflect a simpler style to go with everyday kimono. However, some of the more ornate hanhaba that you will find sewn in the maru style are probably former maru obi recycled into the narrow form. Children's hanhaba are always made of the brightest imaginable colors, with a stenciled pattern rather than elaborate embroidery or weaving.

There are all-black obi and white-on-white obi. These black obi may be made of the finest silk with barely discernible patterns woven into the design. Somber, yet lovely, solid black obi are worn as part of the mourning attire at a funeral or out of respect for the death of a relative.

While white obi are traditionally worn by the bride at her wedding ceremony, before the Taisho era (1912–26), a widow could dress all in white signifying that she would never marry again. Therefore some very old white silk obi may not have been used only for weddings.

In general there is a hierarchy of obi styles based on the type of kimono that can be worn for any given occasion. Most formal are the brocades, metallic or colored, and tapestries, followed in order by dyed silks, woven silks, and non-silk fabrics. As fine obi become more scarce, many of the best are considered collector's items. The most expensive and rare tend to be maru obi, due to their length and width, and also because of their doubled-sided pattern of ornate tapestry or brocade.

Older maru obi are most valuable, as the patina of the gold threads resembles that of an antique tapestry. Newer maru obi, while still beautifully designed and sewn, do not have the luster of the older ones, perhaps due to the use of synthetic fibers in combination with silk fabrics. Brocades, tapestries, and dyed silks are all acceptable for formal wear with the finest kimono, whereas a raw silk, cotton, or wool would be more suitable for everyday wear.

If you are fortunate enough to visit Japan in search of an obi, you can find some lovely designs and top-quality items at any of the local antique shops. You will also be paying top dollar. Some of the large department stores such as Takashimaya and Isetan hold sales several times a year featuring used obi and kimono. Expect to pay several hundred dollars for a typical used obi, whereas a brand new obi can cost several thousand dollars.

For good prices and a selection of older used obi, your best bet would be to visit small shops specializing in used obi and kimono. Other sources include souvenir and gift shops which often carry a few obi. If you happen to visit Tokyo on a weekend, you will want to take advantage of the flea markets and shrine sales held during that time. At these outdoor markets bargaining is acceptable, but don't expect to get a discount at any of the established shops or stores.

Of course outside of Japan it is best to contact a company specializing in obi, although you may stumble on a good deal at any shop dealing in Japanese antiques. An obi dealer may be able to come up with several older obi in similar styles and colors that may be used together if desired. The Japanese sense of color and design is quite different from that of the Western world; some obi color-combinations will appear completely incongruous to the Western eye. Even so, most of the Japanese obi you will see are truly beautiful by any standard.